RISE LIKE A PHOENIX

THE 12 STEPS OF BANKRUPTCY

KATHRYN A. HATHAWAY

Parker House Publishing
www.ParkerHouseBooks.com

This book is designed to provide information and inspiration to our readers. It is sold with the understanding that the publisher and the authors are not engaged in the rendering of psychological, legal, accounting or other professional advice. The content is the sole expression and opinion of the author and not necessarily of the publisher. No warranties or guaranties are expressed or implied by the publisher's choice to include any of the content in this book. Neither the publisher nor the author shall be liable for any physical, psychological, emotional, financial, or commercial damages, including but not limited to special, incidental, consequential or other damages. Our views and rights are the same: You are responsible for your own choices, actions and results.

Book design and cover: Candi Parker

Editing: Teresa Velardi

Published by ParkerHouseBooks.com

Photos licensed from Dreamstime.com/ Rosesonpeach/ Marinini/ Aydindurdu/ Aleka20061

And DollarPhotoClub.com/aitormmfoto/ eelnosiva/ stokkete/ mrallen/ Hogan Imaging/ rocketclips/ wildworx/ 29mokara/ Sergey Nivens

This book is available at quantity discounts for bulk purchases and for branding by businesses and organizations. For further information or to learn more about Being the Phoenix, contact Kathryn@bethephoenix.net.

What People Are Saying...

This book is for anyone who is ready to improve their financial situation and take an honest look at themselves, their finances and their habits to rise and soar as the Phoenix! Kathryn has shared not only her expertise and practical strategies for wading through the troubled waters of financial crisis; she also shares her heart and wisdom to address the emotional impact and undercurrent that creates financial strife. Thank you, Kathryn, for providing a step-by-step road map for people to rise financially and emotionally from the ashes of financial ruin.

Nancy Matthews, International Speaker, Author, Global Leader, Founder of Women's Prosperity Network

With more than 25 years of experience in helping people make their way through bankruptcy, Kathryn Hathaway has brought simplicity to the process. She has brilliantly adapted the 12 Steps for anyone who may have to face the financial music resulting from their spending habits, and shares tools that will help you change your tune from "The Debt I Owe" to "We're in the Money." I highly recommend this book for anyone who is looking to shed some light on their finances.

Teresa Velardi
Author, Editor and Coach
www.transformationaltuesdays.com
www.teresavelardi.com

Dedication

This book is dedicated to all those who have been working hard, doing the best they can and then come to a financial roadblock where they can go no further.

There is a light at the end of the tunnel.
It is not necessarily a train
I believe it is the light of a new day
The light of prosperous tomorrows
It is the light created by the
Phoenix Rising in your Future.

Keep taking that next best step.

As Maya Angelou wrote,

"...and still I rise!"

Acknowledgements

I believe in starting each day with a list of who and what you are grateful for. This morning as I sit with my cats, Xena and Tiger Lily, I'm filled with gratitude for:

Nancy Matthews, Trish Carr and Susan Wiener, the wonderful founding sisters of Women's Prosperity Network (WPN) who over-deliver on their commitment to give women (and the men who "get it") the community, environment, coaching, teaching and skills to bring their dreams and their businesses to life. I'm grateful to my publisher, Candi Parker, of Parker House Publishing who, together with Judee Light, brought WPN to Tallahassee. I'm grateful to my mastermind accountability group, Coach Sandra Hanesworth and partners Gina Edwards, Judy Micale, Lesa Edwards, Vismaya Rubin, Paulina Lopez, and Kevin Taylor (a real man, so cool) who supported and encouraged me by holding the vision of the rising Phoenix.

I'm grateful to Gina Edwards, brilliant creativity coach and editor, who midwifed this book that has been percolating in my mind for nearly 20 years. I'm grateful to Teresa Velardi, the perfect editor at the perfect time with the skills, insight and experience to refine and fan the flame of the rising Phoenix.

I'm grateful to the stellar support in my law firm, paralegal Tara Lareau, who loves our clients and our mission, makes things go smoothly and manages me so well; Sandi Henderson, whose quiet calm efficiency gives everyone confidence that all is well; and Wayne Sprague, our firm's litigation arm, who is as invested in "saving houses and delivering the captive" as I am.

Table of Contents

Introduction

I'd already been practicing bankruptcy law for several years when I was first introduced to the Twelve Steps of AA through a class at church. The twelve-week class was structured so that we would apply those steps to whatever aspect of our life experience seemed unmanageable (how on earth do I choose?) and then study and apply one step each week.

One week per step is hardly enough time to actually experience the depth of growth that can come from really working the steps. However, that relatively short introduction to the Twelve Steps impressed me, as do the people who have diligently followed those steps to rebuild their lives.

I believe that the Twelve Steps of Alcoholics Anonymous are one of the best tools for personal and spiritual growth ever created. They have empowered millions of people to transform from a life that doesn't work to a life that does.

I'm no psychologist. I'm a bankruptcy lawyer. After over twenty-five years of counseling clients who are seeking bankruptcy advice, I have reached two conclusions: 1) debt is addictive; and 2) bankruptcy can be used as an opportunity for personal growth and financial transformation.

Though most people who go through bankruptcy – including myself - stop the process at Step 7 or 8 or 9 of the Twelve Steps, it seems that Steps 8 through 12 have much to offer someone who has filed a bankruptcy. So I decided to continue to work the Twelve Steps post-bankruptcy and to share them with others.

Come walk through the Twelve Steps, adjusted to relate to the bankruptcy process, and see if they speak to you as they speak to me.

The Twelve Steps of Bankruptcy

Modified by the author from the Twelve Steps of Alcoholics Anonymous.

1. We admitted we were powerless over our debt and our spending, and that our lives had become unmanageable.

2. We came to believe that something outside our current knowledge and habitual way of doing things could restore our lives to sanity.

3. We made a decision to turn our will and our financial lives over to this new way of looking at our finances. We agreed to change our ways.

4. Made a searching and fearless inventory of ourselves, our assets and our debts.

5. Admitted to ourselves and to another human being the exact nature of our debts, our assets, and our financial decisions.

6. Were entirely ready to have these defects of character, financial habits and debts removed.

7. Humbly asked for our short-comings and our debts to be removed.

8. Made a list of all persons we had harmed, and became willing to make amends to them all.

9. Made direct amends to said people wherever possible, except when to do so would injure them or others.

10. Continued to take inventory of our financial activities, our debts and our assets, and when we were making financial decisions that did not support our prosperity, promptly admitted it and changed course.

11. Sought through reflection and study, to improve our knowledge of financial management, learning more about good financial stewardship, being careful to act in accordance with our best understanding of those practices.

12. Having had an awakening as the result of these steps, we teach our children and others about financial responsibility, and practice these principles in all our affairs.

Now we begin the flight of the Phoenix – our rise from the ashes of financial ruin into our new financial life!

First Step – I Surrender!

We admitted we were powerless over debt and our spending and that our lives had become unmanageable.

"I need help!" Have you found yourself saying that? How do you know you are powerless over debt? See if any of these situations are familiar to you:

- Are you taking cash advances on your credit cards?

- Are you buying your groceries on credit and then using your grocery money to pay minimum payments on your credit cards?

- Have you ever been tempted to take out a pay-day[i] loan – or worse yet, actually taken such a loan?

- Are you bouncing checks – not just once, but more than once?

- Are you considering taking a loan from your retirement funds to pay off your credit cards?

- Are you considering taking out a second mortgage, or refinancing your home so you can use that money to pay your debt?

- Has one or more of your cars been repossessed?

- Are you hiding a car from the repo man right now?

- Have you pawned your car title so you can pay the dentist?

- Are you waking up in the middle of the night in a cold sweat wondering how you are going to be able to pay the light bill?

- Or if you've already sent the check, are you worried about whether or not it will clear?

- Are you skipping "just one" mortgage payment so you can catch up on all the other little bills?

- Are creditors calling you at home, at work, on your cell phone? Are they calling your family, your neighbors or your employer?

- Are you avoiding the phone because it's probably just another bill collector?

- Is your mail piling up because you don't want to open the bills?

- Are you being sued for a credit card?

- Is your home in foreclosure?

I would suggest to you that if you answer yes to even two of these questions, you already know that your life is unmanageable. You need help! You aren't alone.

Is bankruptcy the best kind of help? Maybe... Maybe not. Are you willing to delve deeper?

Ways we delude ourselves into thinking that we are in control of our finances abound.

Prior to the real estate market crash, my clients Chris and Jane thought they were in control of their consumer spending. They were in control of it because when their credit cards got too high and they couldn't manage their minimum payments, Chris would refinance their home and use the accumulated equity to pay off the cards. Home values were going up fast back then. Though the mortgage payment increased, it was lower than the total of all the minimum payments, and he could afford the payments! Even better, Chris thought, the interest on the mortgage was deductible, making it a double win. Then Chris and Jane would start over again in charging up the credit cards.

Don't Give Away What No One Can Take Away

When Chris and Jane came to see me at my office, they had already refinanced their house and paid off their credit cards at least twice and had run their cards up a third time. I expressed two concerns. First, they were giving away (to credit card companies) what the credit card companies couldn't take away – the equity in their home. In Florida, the equity in your homestead is protected from claims of creditors. The second concern was that if anything happened to Chris' job with the "almost adequate" income, they would lose their house. They wouldn't even be able to sell it to get any money out.

Not wanting to file a bankruptcy, and not being able to admit that his financial plan was creating an unmanageable situation, Chris and Jane decided not to file a bankruptcy, but rather to refinance a third time.

Unfortunately, my second concern is just what happened. The real estate market crashed in 2007 and the value of their house plummeted. Then Chris lost his job in the financial industry because no one was investing any money in retirement.

I learned this because they came back to me to see if they could file a Chapter 13[ii] to save the house. Unfortunately, without Chris' job, there wasn't enough income to create a Chapter 13 plan that would save the house. The house was lost to Chris' previous financial plan.

I'm always looking for a silver lining for my clients. Here, one good thing I could see was that their sons were brilliant, had scholarships to college and the youngest graduated just before the foreclosure sale, so that the loss of the home was not as impactful on their children.

Admitting your life is unmanageable and that you need help early enough so that something constructive can be done is crucial.

Second Step – Let Go

We came to believe that something outside our current knowledge and habitual way of doing things could restore our lives to sanity.

One of the hardest things for people to do is release personal control of their money mess and let someone else look at it. People don't want to believe that anyone else could have done any better with their life situation than they did. Maybe that's true. But, maybe not.

Your own best thinking and planning (or lack thereof) got you to this place. Do you like the scenery? Do you enjoy the sound effects? The ringing phones? The embarrassment? The panic attacks? The worry that your boss will find out? Or that your parents will find out?

I can't tell you how many times I've heard, "If my father

knew I was considering bankruptcy, he'd disown me", "never speak to me again", "be so disappointed in me", "lecture me mercilessly." Is hiding from the situation making your father any less likely to eventually see that you are in trouble?

Are you ready to admit that somebody or something else could take your mess, turn it into order and restore you to sanity?

I have found that, if you really surrender to the bankruptcy process, your life can be transformed. You can be restored to sanity. First, you have to be willing to be transformed.

My client "Laurie" recently shared with me an exciting discovery she made about letting go. After the real estate market crash Laurie lost rental houses, cash flow, and to make matters even worse, her husband died. She had children to support and no means to support them. For the next eight years, Laurie worked retail part-time and created a home based business and paid off her debt a bit at a time. Laurie has integrity and a powerful work ethic - and my admiration.

But because she had no credit, she couldn't expand her business. Finally she went to a bank to see if she could get a small loan and the banker kindly told her that he couldn't loan her any money UNTIL she filed a bankruptcy. So she came to see me.

I know you're asking, what? Bankruptcy a necessity *before* you can get a loan? That's not what anyone would think. But the fact of the matter is that when you are up to your neck in debt, a lender looks at what could happen in the future. The prospective creditor sees that you have a history of unpaid creditors. Why would they lend to you? They also see that any of those previous creditors could sue you and garnish your wages, taking income that you counted on to pay the new creditor. Again, why would they loan to you? After bankruptcy, the new prospective creditor knows that those old creditors can't sue you anymore. They won't be able to get judgments or garnish your wages. Laurie's future banker could see that it was better for his future loan if she discharged (got rid of) her past debt before he loaned her any money.

I looked at Laurie's situation and saw a bankruptcy I wished she had filed years ago. I also saw a wonderful business opportunity for her if she could just expand. We brainstormed different ways of marketing and expanding her business as well as talking about bankruptcy.

Laurie reported that after the idea of bankruptcy had sunk in, she saw that she unconsciously had been holding back in her business and her life because she was afraid that any money she earned would be garnished by her creditors. This is not uncommon. As she let go and started working with the process, other things started happening. I think she found the truth that Goethe voiced two centuries ago:

> "Until one is committed, there is hesitancy, the chance to draw back-- Concerning all acts of initiative (and creation), there is one elementary truth that ignorance of which kills countless ideas and splendid plans: that the moment one definitely commits oneself, then Providence moves too. All sorts of things occur to help one that would never otherwise have occurred. A whole stream of events issues from the decision, raising in one's favor all manner of unforeseen incidents and meetings and material assistance, which no man could have dreamed would have come his way. Whatever you can do, or

dream you can do, begin it. Boldness has genius, power, and magic in it. Begin it now."

~Johann Wolfgang von Goethe (1749-1832)

The big surprise to Laurie was how the Universe stepped in to help her expand once she had let go. A month after she filed her bankruptcy she was offered free office space and a wonderful marketing opportunity to expand her business. She stepped up to accept help in using social media to market her business. We both cried as she shared her expansive vision and experience with me.

When you let go of what's holding you down, you open up the opportunity to actually fly! Laurie is already taking off, her view of the ashes of the past is growing small in the distance.

So, while you are standing at the edge of believing that there might be a better way and that it could restore your life to sanity, decide to do one of the following things:

- Sign up for a debt management course.

- Look online for a credit counseling course.

- Read about debt consolidation programs and maybe even contact one to see what they may be able to do for you and how much they're going to charge. The cost is very important. Very often debt consolidation or debt settlement companies charge more than twice what a Chapter 13 would cost.

- Look online or in the phone book for a reputable bankruptcy lawyer in your area.

- Actually make an appointment with a bankruptcy lawyer. This isn't a commitment to file bankruptcy. You're just doing research. We make our best decisions when we have the most facts.

More and more, clients come to see me after having done considerable research about their options. Good for them! The initial consultation in my office is part of that fact-finding expedition. I strongly encourage you to look at all the options you have. But before you *take any* of the advice all these places give you, make sure you have looked at *all* the options your research uncovers. Look at your life, where you are and where you expect to be in five years. Consider what you need to have in place to be able to get there.

Letting go of personal control should also include talking to an expert. You may have done research on the Internet. That's great. Now you may know something more about finances, than you did before which, of course is very important. I still recommend talking to an expert in the field. Someone who has years of experience working with clients with similar problems may shed a whole new light on possible solutions to your financial dilemma.

I've been working with a client we'll call "Susan." Susan counsels clients on financial matters and has helped many people solve their financial problems. Her own situation however, was so painful to her that she wasn't able to apply her skills to her own finances – particularly her mortgage.

At the top of the real estate market, Susan refinanced her house to take money out to invest in an office building for her own business. After the refinance, she had at least 20% equity in her house and 20% equity in her office building. The interest rate was 6% on the first mortgage and 6.9% on the second. She thought she was pretty well set up.

Then the real estate market crashed. Her house lost about 46% of its value! Her mortgages, which were once 80% of the value of each of the buildings, after the crash were 153% of the value. She was truly, as they say, under water.

If her income had stayed the same she would have been able to continue to pay the mortgages until the market came back. However, Susan was in the financial industry herself and her own income decreased by about 25% with the crash. Susan found herself struggling just like her clients. She was embarrassed. So embarrassed in fact, she chose not to seek outside experts to help her see her own problem more clearly. Susan filed for relief in bankruptcy, but it didn't solve all her financial problems. Lawsuits stopped. She still had mortgages to pay. Even though she knew a lot about finances, without talking about her situation with another professional, Susan missed the benefit of the intelligence that arises when two or more people are sharing information and looking at a problem from different angles. Napoleon Hill calls this the "Mastermind" in his famous bestselling book, *Think and Grow Rich*.

Fast forward eight years. Her income hadn't improved much, but she was muddling along. But because of her aversion to looking at her own situation, Susan didn't even know her own numbers – values of properties, balances of mortgages or what current interest rates were.

Finally she decided that she could no longer tell her clients that they should look honestly at their financial situations and take steps to improve them unless she, herself was willing to consult an expert about her *own* situation.

Susan did a little online research and thought that a Home Affordable Refinance Program (HARP)[iii] mortgage modification might now be a possibility. She didn't try it when they first came out because her mortgages were 153% of the then value and HARP refinances were, she thought, limited to 125%.

So she took a deep breath and contacted a mortgage broker who walked her through finding out what her current numbers were.

1. The new value of her home, based on Zillow.com had come up almost 25% from the low point in 2013. That was a pleasant surprise. Hope flickered in her heart!

2. Balances due on her first and second mortgages were now 120% of the home value rather than the 153% just 2.5 years earlier.

3. Best of all, HARP regulations had changed and they would now refinance up to 200% of value of her home. Not that it would necessarily be a good idea, but it opened windows of possibility.

The mortgage broker also told her that her mortgage was a Freddie Mac mortgage and she was eligible for a HARP refinance of her first mortgage, even though the HARP mortgage would not touch her second mortgage. Still, lowering the payment on the first mortgage made the second mortgage more affordable.

Susan learned all this within a half an hour of making the phone call to an expert who could help her. Letting go of control of her problem and consulting an expert had given her hope and the possibility of an answer.

Anyone's life can become unmanageable for a time. Doctors can become ill. Lawyers can be sued. Coaches may need coaching. Financial professionals can make decisions that will cost them money. We can all benefit from knowledge outside that which we already have, and that new knowledge can help us return our lives to sanity.

Third Step – I Decide

We made a decision to turn our will and our financial lives over to this new way of looking at our finances. We agreed to change our ways.

Having decided that your life was unmanageable in taking Step One then finally having researched many options and decided that just maybe, another method could restore your life to sanity when you took Step Two, you now decide to turn your will over to this new way of thinking. This new way of thinking may include the bankruptcy process. You agree to change. But before you actually agree, you might have a few questions.

Just as you might ask in your first AA meeting,

- Can I have a glass of champagne at a wedding?

- What if I can have just one beer and stop?

- Once I get this poison out of my system, can I go back to moderate social drinking?

You ask your bankruptcy lawyer to see if you can fit your old habits into this new way of doing things.

Q: Can I keep just one credit card through the bankruptcy for emergencies?

A: Probably not. Even if you don't have a balance on the card, most credit card companies subscribe to a service or program that tells them when one of their card holders files a bankruptcy, and then they cancel the card(s.)

Q: Before I file bankruptcy, can I transfer the car I own free and clear to my brother for $1. Then after the bankruptcy he can sell it back to me for $1 so my creditors won't get it?

A: No, you can't! That would be considered a fraudulent transfer[1]or bankruptcy fraud. If you transferred the car to your brother and then filed a bankruptcy, the best outcome you could expect would be for the bankruptcy trustee to go to your brother and say, give me the car so I can sell it and use the money to pay this joker's creditors! If there had been an exemption for some of the equity in the car available to you, you would have lost that exemption.

Worse, though, if you didn't report that transfer in your bankruptcy paperwork and the trustee finds out about it, which is easy for them to do since so much property ownership information is easily available online, the trustee

---

[1] 11 U.S.C. §§ 544, 548.

might also report your fraudulent transfer to the United States Department of Justice. You could be criminally prosecuted for bankruptcy fraud for lying in your bankruptcy schedules. You could spend some time in federal prison. Trust me; there is always some "little birdie" around to tattle on you to your bankruptcy trustee. I see it all the time.

Q: Can I sell my car prior to filing bankruptcy and use it to pay my mom back the $20,000 she loaned me last year?

A: Probably not. If you aren't paying your other creditors and "prefer" to pay your mother, that's called a "preferential transfer to an insider".[2] If you file a bankruptcy within one year of repaying your mother, the bankruptcy trustee would have the right to go to your mother and say, "That money Sonny Boy gave you 6 months ago? He should have given it to me so I could pay his creditors who don't love him as much as you do. Give me the money." Christmas dinners may become very unpleasant if mom has to turn the money over to the trustee. Of course, you might argue that Christmas dinners would be unpleasant if you didn't pay mom back at all. I understand your argument. But hopefully Mom is understanding and loves you. The Bankruptcy Court is not.

Q: What if I sold my car prior to filing bankruptcy and used the money to pay the child support judgment I owe my ex-wife?

A: Check with your bankruptcy lawyer first. By now, you probably recognize that this is another preferential transfer – preferring your ex-wife over other creditors, but it would

___

[2] 11 U.S.C. § 542

be a preferential transfer to a creditor that would stand first in line anyway. Domestic support obligations are the number one priority in Section 507 of the Bankruptcy Code. "Women and children" are finally first! But before you do that, check with your bankruptcy lawyer. Your lawyer has experience in these matters and also has some perspective on your financial situation that you don't have. There could be legal and practical reasons for not doing that.

Q: Before filing bankruptcy could I put the money from the sale of my car into an exempt asset – one that the law prevents my creditors and the bankruptcy Trustee from taking when I file bankruptcy? I've heard that my IRA, paid for life insurance policies, annuities and more things are protected from creditor's claims.

A: It is true that in most jurisdictions assets such as those you mention are safe from your creditors. But transferring money that your creditors are entitled to be paid from such as the money from the sale of your car, into an exempt asset such as life insurance policy or an IRA is a "fraudulent conversion" of an asset.

The bankruptcy trustee can then undo any of those transfers and use the money to pay your creditors.

Q: Before I file the bankruptcy, could I use the money from the car to pay down my home mortgage? I understand my homestead is exempt from creditors' claims.

A: All 50 states exempt some portion of your home from claims of creditors. It sounds like a good idea to pay down your mortgage to take full advantage of the homestead exemption prior to filing bankruptcy, but it may be considered a "fraudulent conversion." In some states a bankruptcy trustee may be able to get that money back out of your house.

Q: Do I *really* have to list everything I own? Even that car Dad gave me that I never registered in my name?

A: Yes. You must list everything you own, whether that ownership is legal (having the title in your name) or equitable (you paid for it, but it's in someone else's name.) To do any less is "bankruptcy fraud" and you don't even want to think about going there. The United States Attorney's office is on the lookout for situations like this so they can make an example for other people thinking they can lie on their bankruptcy schedules. Honest mistakes can usually be fixed, but hiding assets intentionally? Not so easy.

If you make any transfers or conversions of assets at all in the two years prior to filing bankruptcy, you must report that transfer to your creditors and your bankruptcy trustee in your bankruptcy paperwork.

So for instance, the $3500 you paid for that car that isn't in your name would have to be reported in your schedules as a transfer of money. Failure to list that transfer of money AND the car would be two lies and more definite proof of intention to defraud your creditors. And these failures are easy for a trustee to catch as they review your bank statements, paychecks and the public records. And then there's always the "little birdie" that calls the Trustee to inform on you.

I'm sure you have heard the definition of insanity? Doing the same thing over and over again and expecting to get different results? Remember, our own best thinking got us

21

where we are. Deciding to turn our will and our financial life over to a new way of looking at things is crucial. Asking questions is an important part of learning, but the bottom line in this process of transformation and the bottom line of this Third Step is "We agreed to change our ways." Welcome to financial life transformation!

Fourth Step – Inventory of Debts & Assets

Made a searching and fearless moral inventory of
ourselves and our assets and our debts.

This step is parallel to completing a bankruptcy petition or questionnaire. My understanding of the "fearless and searching moral inventory" made in AA is that you include not only your debts – things that you have done wrong in your addiction that hurt someone, but you also list your assets – things about you that are good. In order to begin to change, you have to know who and where you are; the good, the bad and the ugly. We all have some of each. We just have to look at it...fearlessly!

This is now the time to list your debts. We divide them into categories:

Priority debts: Most common priority debts include:

- Past due child support or alimony.

- Taxes – let your bankruptcy lawyer help you determine whether all the taxes you may owe are priority. Some are and contrarily, some aren't.

- Wages owed to another person for work done in the last 60 days.

- Deposits you are holding for someone else, such as rent deposits (aka security deposits) if you have rental properties, or a deposit someone made on work you were doing for them and haven't yet completed.

- Damages caused in an accident where you were under the influence of an intoxicant. These debts are also not dischargeable. So if you file a bankruptcy with such a debt, you will very likely have that debt after your other debts are discharged.

Secured debts: A secured debt is one that is attached to an asset such as the mortgage on your house, the lien on your car, the money Best Buy loaned you on your Best Buy credit card to purchase that fancy new television in your living room. If you want to keep the asset, you need to pay it in some way. We'll talk about those options later.

Unsecured debts: The vast majority of your other debt is general unsecured nonpriority including credit cards, medical bills, the loan from "Bank of Mom & Dad", student loans. Once again, student loans are usually not discharged in bankruptcy, so after your bankruptcy you will still owe the student loans.

If you don't know what category something goes in, write **it down under your best guess for a category. Your lawyer can rearrange the categories once you give him/her the** information. You or your attorney might want to run a tri-merge credit report to make sure that all reported debts are in the petition and are naming correctly the current owner of that debt. A tri-merge credit report is one includes debt from the three credit reporting agencies – Experian, Equifax and Transunion. Your lawyer can't possibly know you owe Mom and Dad or Aunt Sally if you don't tell her, since they obviously don't report to the credit bureaus. It is your *legal* obligation to list those debts too.

Assets: The Inventory does not stop there. You must also list everything you own or have an equity interest in. So you list:

- Bank accounts

- Household goods

- Collections (aka Accounts Receivable)

- Jewelry

- Clothing

- Sports equipment

- Insurance policies

- Annuities

- Retirement accounts
- Inheritances that are pending (the person already died)

- Tax refunds

- Money people owe you including alimony and child support

- Rights you have to sue other people whether you have already sued them, are waiting to sue them or decided not to sue, as well as any known possible upcoming settlement

- Business inventory and equipment that belongs to you

- Vehicles

- Boats

- Airplanes

- Farming equipment

- Crops

- Animals

- Every other thing under the sun

Bankruptcy trustees are very good at doing research. Assume that everything you own or could own is easily viewable on the Internet; because it is.

You must also value your "stuff" fairly and accurately. According to the Bankruptcy Code, the value of property is what you would have to pay to purchase that property in its used condition from a seller of similar goods.

Generally accepted accounting principles (GAAP) do not govern the value of property in a bankruptcy case. So just because you have fully depreciated a piece of business property does not mean that it is valueless in a bankruptcy case. The value is what you would have to pay to buy something just like it in similar condition from someone who sells like goods.

Value sometimes means what you could get for it at a garage sale, because resale stores would not accept that particular thing. Believe it or not there are some things that even Goodwill won't take. Sometimes value means what you'd pay for it on EBay or at a pawn shop. Your opinion of value is usually good enough so long as you have done some reasonable research.

Unless you recently purchased the item, what you paid for it is not the value of the thing now. Note the difference between "new" and "used."

Income and Expenses

Your creditors have a right to know how much income you make from all sources. Even if a portion of your income is tax free such as VA Disability Benefits or Social Security or from child support or alimony. List it all. You may have heard that Social Security is considered "non-countable income" under the Bankruptcy Code, and that is true. List it anyway.

Your expenses – where you actually spend your money will probably be a revelation. I have found over the last 25+

years that my clients have no real idea what it costs them to live. This arises from two causes: 1) they don't want to look; and 2) they've been using credit cards for many expenses and then counting minimum credit card payments as part of their budget.

I recommend that once my clients have committed to filing a bankruptcy, they should stop using and stop paying their credit cards if they haven't already. This will give you a month or two to put all income and all expenses through one checking account. This is sometimes the very first time my clients get a clear picture of what they actually have in the way of income and expenses.

Married couples need to do the same. All the money deposited into one account and all the expenses paid from that one account. So many of my married clients come to me with separate accounts and then contribute a portion of their income to overhead after they have paid their personal expenses. This is not a recipe for financial success for the family. One partner often gets their needs taken care of and the other partner is left holding the bag. Not fair. Not teamwork. Not marriage and definitely not a good way to maintain a household budget.

The bankruptcy system presumes that married people are a true economic unit. All for one and one for all. Even if only one of the couple is filing bankruptcy, all the income must be shown as available to pay all the living expenses and obligations of the marital economic unit. (Sounds romantic, doesn't it?) All income and expenses of both parties to the marriage are reported in the schedules and on the Means Test. I urge you to look at this and see how you could improve the teamwork in your marriage. Working together like this actually improves intimacy.

For more intense discussion about budgeting, see the Tenth Step section on budgeting and the Appendix which sets out guidelines for creating your new financial plan for rising from the ashes of your financial ruin.

Statement of Financial Affairs

The remaining part of the fearless and searching moral and financial inventory is the Statement of Financial Affairs. This requests your financial history.

- How much money have you made over the past three years from employment or operation of your business?

- How much money have you received from other sources in the last three years? This includes life insurance, inheritance, workers' compensation, unemployment compensation benefits, disability benefits, Social Security benefits, child support or alimony, even regular support from family members. They want to know how you have been surviving.

- What creditors have you paid and how much in the last 90 days?

- Have you paid back an "insider" – business partner or family member – in the last year?

- What lawsuits have you been involved in during the past twelve months?

- Has anything been repossessed, garnished, seized or sold at foreclosure sale in the last year?

- Has any of your property been assigned for the benefit of creditors in the last year?

- Have you made any extraordinary gifts (more than $600 to family or a charity) in the last year?

- Have you had any losses from fire, theft, gambling, miscellaneous slip and fall, dog bite or car accident in the last year?

- What have you paid to anyone for bankruptcy advice or debt management advice in the last year?

- Have you sold, transferred or given away any money or property in the last 2 years?

- Have you closed any financial accounts in the last year?

- Do you have a safe deposit box or storage unit? If so, what's in it?

- Has your bank taken any money out of your account in the last 90 days because you owed them money, but without your permission? (Example: did you skip a car or credit card payment so you could pay the light bill but then find that the bank had taken your car or credit card payment out of your account with them anyway?)

- All of your addresses over the last three years.

- Do you hold or control property that belongs to anyone else? This could be your mother's dining room set that you're holding for her. It could also be having your name on your mom's bank account so you can pay her bills for her.

- Have you been married or divorced in a community property state in the last 8 years? (New York, California, Louisiana, Arizona, Idaho, Nevada, New Mexico, Texas, Washington and Wisconsin are community property states – states in which assets and debts of married people are controlled by a different set of laws that come into play in the bankruptcy arena.)

- Have you been informed that you are the "proud owner" of environmentally hazardous property?

- Have you owned more than 5% interest in a business in the last 4 years? And if so, more business information is required.

These questions are important.

Suppose that before you talked to a bankruptcy lawyer, you transferred some land to your boyfriend so your creditors wouldn't get it. Then you have your first consultation with your bankruptcy lawyer who tells you not to transfer any property away, so of course you tell him about the land you gave to your boyfriend. Your lawyer says,

"You can't do that! Transfer it back!" So you do. Your obligation in your bankruptcy schedules is to disclose both the transfer to your boyfriend and the transfer back.

Your bankruptcy schedules must be prepared accurately and carefully. Don't take them casually and don't trust a lawyer who seems to take it casually. It all matters. The truth matters. Your reputation and your personal integrity matter.

If you have historically earned a lot of money and bought nice furniture and things, or if you just don't know *how* to value your furniture, I recommend that you hire an auctioneer or appraiser to do it for you. This will prevent you from over-valuing your property as well as undervaluing. On more than one occasion, I have had a client bring me their list of property, which they valued themselves, and I told them they needed to hire an appraiser, because their values were too high.

For instance, "George" had inherited his mother's furniture, which was very heavy solid wood and in his mind worth a fortune. He brought me a list of his property with values he came up with himself. The values he estimated made his mother's furniture alone come up to $14,000 – and his other furniture added another $8000 to that. In Florida, he could only keep $1000 worth of personal property which meant that he would be either paying his creditors $21,000 to keep that furniture or he would have to turn over the furniture he held so dear to the Bankruptcy Trustee for her to sell and use the money to pay his creditors pennies on the dollar.

I suspected that he had confused sentimental value with monetary value, so I gave him the name and number of the Trustee's bankruptcy auctioneer to hire to do an appraisal of his personal property. His $500 investment in the appraisal saved him thousands of dollars.

George was mildly insulted that his mother's beautiful, but very dark, heavy and out of date and not very "Florida" furniture was only worth about $4,000 – and the remainder of his furniture only worth another $2,000. In order to buy back his furniture from the bankruptcy estate, he only had to pay the Trustee $5,000, which was much more manageable than $21,000.

Honesty is always the best policy. If you need help in determining values or completing your respective lists in this all important step, ask for it. Your attorney is there to help you to gain clarity and to help you make the most out of the process so that you can have a fresh start as you will surely discover in the next step.

Taking our own inventory is supposed to be fearless according to the Fourth Step. This step is initially approached with dread by people in any Twelve Step program. We dread looking at ourselves under a magnifying glass. You can't eliminate something in your life that doesn't work for you unless you know it's there. As our lives became more and more unmanageable, we all ignored our budget, our bills, and our assets. I encourage you to approach Step Four with the understanding that in knowledge there is truth, and in truth there is freedom.

Rise Like a Phoenix

Fifth Step – Confess to Your Lawyer

Admitted to ourselves and to another human being,
the exact nature of our debts, our assets and
our financial decisions.

The next step in the bankruptcy process involves revealing your assets and liabilities, budget and financial history to your bankruptcy lawyer. Your lawyer should ask you questions about the information you gathered and ask other questions related to the information requested in the bankruptcy petition.

Most often, in this appointment the client tells me about something that they didn't write down. "I didn't think that counted." Or "I didn't think I had to write down that car because it is paid for."

Your bankruptcy lawyer cannot tell you how bankruptcy laws will affect you unless she knows about all your assets as well as all your debts, your income and your expenses. They also need your financial history to make sure there aren't any transfers in your past that will give you trouble in your bankruptcy.

As my old Contracts teacher, Professor McHugh often said, "A shot glass full of facts is worth a tub full of law." In other words, all the law your lawyer knows is worth nothing if she doesn't know your facts.

Bankruptcy is a game played with the cards face up. You don't keep secrets from your bankruptcy lawyer or from the Court. Your lawyer can help you deal with anything as long as you tell him/her the truth. Giving misinformation to the Court under penalty of perjury is serious business.

To illustrate the importance of confessing everything – every asset and every debt – to your lawyer, I'm sharing the following story – a real case published in the Federal Reporters published by Thomson West Publishing as *Reed v. City of Arlington*, 650 F.3d 551 (5th Cir. 2011.)

A firefighter, Kim Lubke, and his wife filed a bankruptcy. They neglected to list or tell their lawyer about an asset – a $1 million judgment Mr. Lubke had obtained against the City of Arlington. They had also neglected to list the attorney fees owed to the attorney who represented them in the suit against the City. The apparent reason for these two omissions was to keep the $1 million judgment a secret from the bankruptcy court. If they listed the attorney fees to their lawyer, the attorney as an officer of the Court would have had had to let the bankruptcy trustee know about the asset. Initially the Lubke's snuck it through and received a bankruptcy discharge and a ruling that they had no assets.

In the meantime, the judgment Mr. Lubke won against the City of Arlington was being appealed up through the Federal Court system. The appellate court affirmed the judgment, but said that the damages needed to be recalculated. In the course of the negotiating the damages, Lubke's attorney learned about the bankruptcy and contacted the bankruptcy trustee.

Ms. Reed, the Chapter 7 trustee, immediately reopened the bankruptcy case, had the Lubke's discharge revoked for their bad faith failure to disclose, and entered into settlement negotiations directly with the City of Arlington. Her goal was to get enough to pay the creditors in full and to pay the expenses of litigation. In a normal Chapter 7, where the Debtor had disclosed this asset in his bankruptcy schedules, the Trustee would have gotten as much as she could and the balance remaining after paying all his creditors would then be distributed to Mr. Lubke.

Here, however, there is a legal principle called "judicial estoppel" which basically means that a litigant is "estopped" (fancy word for "prevented") from claiming in one court what he denies in another court. Here, Mr. Lubke denied to the bankruptcy court that anyone owed him money or that he had any claim that anyone owed him money. The City argued that because he had lied to the bankruptcy court about the judgment, he was "estopped" or prevented from claiming payment on the judgment after the bankruptcy. The trustee argued that she and the creditors were innocent of any wrongdoing, and that she should be allowed to go forward in collecting the judgment for the benefit of the creditors.

The court crafted a clever solution. The judge ruled that the Trustee was allowed to collect money from the City of Arlington, to pay it out to creditors and to pay her fees. Any money that was left over was to be returned to the City, rather than to Mr. Lubke, who due to his bad faith actions, was not entitled to get anything at all.

That was a huge price to pay for withholding information! Always tell the truth to your lawyer and the Court. Your lawyer cannot help you get the best result possible if you don't disclose *everything*.

In Twelve Step programs, the best way to work them is to have a sponsor – someone who helps us look at our "stuff" from another point of view, who helps us see more clearly, and who guides us with their experience. In the bankruptcy process, our attorney is our sponsor. The fearless and searching inventory of our debts, assets and history and then confessing everything to our lawyer helps us see our "stuff" more clearly. Things you may not have seen as assets are revealed as assets. Things we may want to hide could turn out to be assets that are exempt so no one can take away from us anyway. Sharing all this information with our lawyer is essential to creating documents we will be signing under penalty of perjury and submitting to the Court. And as we have just seen, confessing it all to our lawyer could keep us out of jail.

Sixth Step – Being Ready

*Were entirely ready to have these defects of character,
financial habits and debts removed.*

What does being "entirely ready" mean?

One of the ways of being entirely ready is being aware of and accepting of the consequences. To other people, it means just close your eyes, plug your nose and jump! I've filed many bankruptcies for people who took the "close your eyes..." readiness position. Sometimes they had a foreclosure sale pending the next day and were willing to deal with whatever the consequences of filing bankruptcy would be for them later, so long as they could stop the sale of their house today.

For people who have a little more time available, I recommend that they consider what the side effects of filing bankruptcy are and decide whether they can live with them, and how they are going to deal with them.

As a consequence of filing bankruptcy you may find:

1. You can't get an FHA, Freddie Mac, or Fannie Mae mortgage on a house for least 2 or 3 years after receiving your bankruptcy discharge. Conventional mortgages – 4 years!

2. It is very difficult to obtain credit cards with a reasonable interest rate. Some credit cards are available if you pay a large annual fee and high interest rates. A better choice would be secured credit cards, where you open a savings account and deposit 110% of the card limit in the account. To reestablish other credit you need to be able to show responsible use of a major credit card. This will do it.

3. Vehicle loans are available, but at least until you have created a record of responsible credit use, the rates are high. You may have to drive your old car for a while – in fact, I recommend it. My own car is now 12 years old, paid for and I still love it.

4. Often potential new creditors will require an explanation about your bankruptcy and why you filed it. Make your story short and true: "I got divorced"; "I had a period of unemployment;" "Business slowed down with the economy and my business failed." Whatever it is, get comfortable telling it. You may have to tell it often.

5. A Chapter 7 bankruptcy will be on your credit report for 10 years after you receive your discharge.

6. A Chapter 13 bankruptcy will be on your credit report for 7 years after you receive your discharge.

7. Your bankruptcy filing may appear in the newspaper of your town.

8. Your bankruptcy filing is a matter of public record, and people could get access to your bankruptcy schedules, see what you own and its value, and who you owe and how much you owe. They will even be able to see what your income was over the last couple of years. You need to come to terms with that before you actually file.

9. If you become eligible to inherit from someone or to receive life insurance in the 180 days after your bankruptcy is filed, that property becomes property of your bankruptcy estate and will be used by the Trustee of your bankruptcy to pay your creditors. This doesn't mean that you can protect the inheritance by asking the executor to just hold the money until your bankruptcy is over. Inheritance vests (becomes yours under the law) when your loved one dies.

10. If you had the right to sue a person or a company for something, such as a car accident or employment discrimination, your right to sue, and the money you get from the suit is property of the bankruptcy estate. You won't get any of the proceeds unless there is something left over after your creditors and administrative expenses of the Trustee are paid. Remember the fate of Mr. Lubke in the previous chapter. Do not try to hide the right to sue from the bankruptcy court. If you tell your lawyer about the asset, your lawyer may advise you not to file the bankruptcy at all.

You need to be willing to deal with these inconveniences if you want to file a bankruptcy. And you need to weigh them against the benefits.

By now, you may have forgotten what the benefits of filing bankruptcy are! Let me remind you.

1. Lawsuits against you stop.

2. Foreclosures stop – at least for a while – giving you a chance to rehabilitate the mortgage, apply for modification or even move.

3. Garnishments of your bank accounts and your wages stop.

4. You will be able to answer the phone again. By law, your creditors must stop calling.

5. You will be able to answer the door without worrying that there's a process server at the door.

6. You will be able to rebuild your credit again. Remember, if you haven't been paying your bills and people have been suing you, your credit was already trash, and you were already unable to get loans to buy a house, car or get new credit cards. Bankruptcy isn't going to make it any worse.

7. Credit scores often go UP after a bankruptcy discharge is entered!

8. Creditors who wouldn't give you credit prior to your bankruptcy filing are now more likely to give you credit because a) you can't file bankruptcy again for a

long time; and b) the old creditors on your credit report can no longer sue you and make claim on the income that you would be using to pay the new creditor, so you are now a better risk.

9. You do not suffer the tax consequences of creditors forgiving debt. Cancelled debt becomes taxable income under the Income Tax Code. But not if you discharged that debt in bankruptcy.

10. You can use your income to invest in your future instead of continuing to pay for your past.

After you have made a thorough cost benefit analysis, you will be able to knowingly "become willing" to have your debts removed.

Mandatory Credit Counseling

Another part of the consequences of filing bankruptcy is that you must take the mandatory credit counseling required under the Bankruptcy Abuse Prevention and Consumer Protection Act of 2005 (BAPCPA.) Fortunately, this hour and a half to two-hour class is offered online and by phone. The online class is by far the preferable way to go as you can stop and start as it is convenient for you. The telephone class must be done in one sitting.

Congress created this prerequisite because the banking lobbyists convinced them that people were filing bankruptcy who didn't actually need to file. They thought that somehow this required course would put a barrier between consumers and their ability to file an emergency bankruptcy.

You can look at the mandatory course as a barrier to filing, but really it is a benefit, a learning opportunity that only takes an hour and a half or two hours of your time. It's great information that will help you to better manage your money after the bankruptcy is over.

In the Sixth Step I invite you to imagine what your life will be like in a future without cement overshoes impeding your every forward step. Be ready to release the things that don't work for you, so you can fill your life with what does. Imagine yourself standing at the edge of all that you know, ready to fly like the seagull in the picture at the beginning of this chapter. Imagine the thrill of unfettered flight into your new life. Come on up! The weather is fine!

Let's conclude this chapter with some inspiration for you to take with you for the rest of your journey through the steps.

"We can lift ourselves out of ignorance; we can find ourselves to be creatures of excellence, intelligence and skill. We can be free!"
~ Richard Bach – Jonathan Livingston Seagull

Seventh Step – Filing the Bankruptcy Petition

Humbly asked for our short-comings and our
debts to be removed.

You would think that if someone went through all the trouble to list their debts and assets, reveal their financial history to an attorney, and actually sign a petition, that filing the petition would be automatic. Not so. I have many signed petitions in my "in process" drawer. Actually pulling the trigger is a separate step, and not everyone is ready to do it.

The bankruptcy petition reads:

> **I declare under penalty of perjury that the information provided in this petition is true and correct...**
> **I request relief in accordance with the chapter of title 11, United States Code, specified in this petition.**
>
> **X_____Date:_____ [3]**

The Catholic catechism contains psychological genius –

---

[3] Official Form 1, U.S. Bankruptcy Rules and Forms.

whether you are a practicing Catholic or practicing atheist. Part of that genius is the realization that confessing your sins and then dwelling on them is simply not healthy. You have to take the next step and actually ASK for forgiveness. The priest then says, "You are forgiven" and prescribes penance that you must perform. The penance isn't for God or the priest; it's for you, to help you get right with having done something that doesn't work. Likewise, in the Twelve Steps, you humbly ask for your short-comings to be removed.

In the bankruptcy world, the filing of the bankruptcy petition is the request that the debts be removed. Then there's penance. Penance includes:

1. Mandatory attendance at a Meeting of Creditors between 20 and 40 days after the petition is filed. At this meeting your trustee asks you questions under oath about your financial affairs. Creditors receive notice of this meeting and have the right to be there to ask questions. In usual cases, no one is there. However sometimes the United States Trustee's Office has a representative at the meeting, or the secured creditor on your car loan, if local, will be there to see if you intend to reaffirm the car loan. In rare cases, if you are in the middle of a lawsuit, the other side's lawyer will send a representative to ask you questions. More often than not, it will be you and the trustee at that meeting.

2. After the meeting is concluded your creditors and the trustee have 30 days in which they can object to your claimed exemptions. For instance, if you claimed a homestead exemption on a house and someone thinks

you don't really live there, they might object to your homestead exemption.

3. The trustee and creditors have 60 days after the creditors meeting is concluded in which they can object to the dischargeability of one or more of your debts or object to your receiving a discharge at all. Objection to discharge of a debt might occur if the debt arose under one of the circumstances listed in 11 U.S.C. § 523.[4]

Process aside, to be discharged from your debts, you actually have to *humbly* ask for these debts to be removed as instructed by the Seventh Step. You must file the petition with the Court.

---

[4] Under § 523, some of the listed debts are nondischargeable in Chapter 7 without a court order specifically saying so. Taxes are nondischargeable under § 523(a)(1) if they were incurred in returns that were not filed at all, or were filed within the last two years, or that were for taxes that were due within the previous 3 years OR were incurred due to fraudulent returns. Also nondischargeable in Chapter 7 without court hearing are alimony, child support and debts that were incurred to a spouse or child pursuant to a marital settlement agreement or court order in the course of a divorce under state law. § 523(a)(5) and (a)(15.) Others listed in § 523 might be discharged in a Chapter 7 if no one files a petition within 60 days of the creditors' meeting to have the court declare the debts nondischargeable. Those debts include debts incurred by fraud; credit card charges for luxuries or cash advances on cards that were incurred close to the time of the bankruptcy; debts that weren't listed in the bankruptcy; fraud of a fiduciary; willful or malicious injury to another person; debt for fine penalty or forfeiture within 3 years of filing the bankruptcy; most student loans; damages for death or personal injury incurred when the debtor was driving while under the influence of drugs or alcohol; debts that the debtor couldn't discharge in a previous bankruptcy and many other that rarely are seen in a consumer bankruptcy. Please see 11 U.S.C. § 523 for a complete listing.

Rise Like a Phoenix

Eighth Step – The Fork in the Road - Chapter 7's Statement of Intentions or Chapter 13 Plan

Made a list of all persons we had harmed, and became willing to make amends to them all.

You may wonder, "How does becoming willing to make amends" fit into bankruptcy if the whole idea of bankruptcy is to get rid of debt so that you can move forward and build a better life. How can becoming willing to make amends to them square with building a future?

Amends in the bankruptcy context, starts with acknowledging that we owed these people and companies money. Most of our debts arose because these people and companies trusted us to pay them back. They extended us credit and we accepted the money or goods they gave us.

For consumers, there are two kinds of bankruptcy:

Chapter 7 liquidation bankruptcy, which is over in 100 days or so; and the Chapter 13 wage earners debt consolidation which is more like consumer credit counseling on steroids.

In Chapter 7, the bankruptcy petition includes a Statement of Intentions where you listed your secured creditors such as your mortgage on your house or your car loan, or the purchase money security interest you have in the computer you purchased at Best Buy on your Best Buy credit card and stated how you wanted to treat them.

For instance, if you have a car loan, you could say that you intend to surrender your car back to the bank. You could intend to "reaffirm" the debt – promise to pay just as if you never filed a bankruptcy. You could intend to "redeem" the car. What's that? Section 722 of the Bankruptcy Code lets debtors redeem collateral from the secured creditor for fair market value. How does it work? Let's say that you owe the bank $20,000 for a car that is now worth $10,000. This might happen when you had traded in a car that was worth less than you owed and then put the difference into the next car you bought. You like the car, but you can't afford to pay $20,000 for it and still get your "fresh start" in bankruptcy. So you use the procedure under Section 722 to pay the bank $10,000 for the car. Where do you get the $10,000? You might be able to take the money out of an exempt asset such as an IRA to pay off the bank. Or you could borrow the money from a lender that specializes in lending to debtors in bankruptcy for just such purposes. Or maybe you have a family member who could help you.

Another way the "willingness to make amends" shows up in Chapter 7 is when you have nonexempt assets that must be turned over to the Trustee for liquidation so the Trustee can pay your creditors who file claims. Sometimes those assets include the proceeds of a lawsuit or claim you had against someone else or money you inherited. That money goes to pay your creditors. My clients have varying degrees of willingness from "That's not fair!" to "If I'd gotten that money before I'd filed I would have used the money to pay debts anyway."

In a Chapter 13, amends means creating the Plan. This plan is a 3 to 5-year contract between you and your creditors saying how you intend to pay them back at least a portion of what you owe. Chapter 13 plans are a powerful way to take back control of your finances, save homes, sometimes refinance cars and get rid of unsecured debt. There will be more about Chapter 13 under the Ninth Step. Finally, after your bankruptcy is over, as you review your bankruptcy creditor schedules (Schedules D, E, and F) you might want to look at other creditors you could make amends to without breaking the bank.

- If you included an overdraft or bounced check to your banking institution in your list of debts (you are required to list all debts you owe, remember) you should consider making amends to the banking institution or person to whom you wrote the bad check. Writing checks for insufficient funds is an actual crime and filing bankruptcy does not erase it. This does not include payday loans, however. A check written to a payday loan place is a promissory note – a promise to pay in the future. It is different from a check because a check is a commitment to pay right now. The payday loan lender knows that your check is not good now, therefore writing that check is not a crime. It's not a good idea, but it's not a crime.

- What about the little guy? Like your yard man, or your dentist, or your electrician. The small business people really suffer when they aren't paid for work they did. The big banks have an anticipated budget item for losses due to personal bankruptcy. Your lawn man doesn't. As you can afford it, you might become willing to make amends to some of these folks.

In considering a "willingness to make amends", imagine winning the lottery! If you won the lottery, could you imagine being *willing* to pay the creditors back? I may be giving willingness to make amends short shrift, but I think if you just got to this point of being willing to pay them if you won the lottery, you would have made a good first pass on the Eighth Step.

So I recommend that you make a list of people to whom you will make amends. Include the car payment and mortgage payment you are going to make. If you want to pay back a family loan after your bankruptcy is over, put that on the list too.

The Eighth Step does not require us to do anything except make the list and become willing to make the amends, however that may look. The actual making of the amends or taking action on our list is in the Ninth Step, so let's be sure not to jump ahead of ourselves. Simply make the list. It may even take some time to become willing to make the amends after the list is made, so let's agree to stay with this step until we are ready to move forward. There is no finish line to race to.

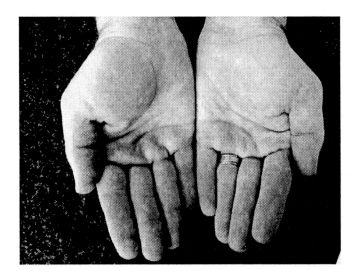

Ninth Step – Reaffirmation, Redemption, Surrender OR the Chapter 13 Plan

Made direct amends to said people wherever possible, except when such amends would injure them or others.

How we make direct amends is by acting on the intentions we made in the Eighth Step in our Statement of Intentions, or making payments to the Chapter 13 Trustee and other creditors as you mapped out in your Chapter 13 Plan.

One way of making amends is the surrender of collateral back to the creditor so the creditor can re-sell it and use that money to satisfy your debt.

In Chapter 7, another way would be to decide to retain and pay for some items. For instance: your car loan. You like your car, it is in good condition, you can afford the monthly payment and the car is worth what you owe on it or more, so you "reaffirm" the loan. Reaffirm means to promise to pay the loan just as if you had never filed a bankruptcy. To do this you and your creditor sign a Reaffirmation Agreement which is filed with the Court. After the bankruptcy is discharged, if you don't pay the loan, the creditor could repossess the car and sue you for the difference between the note and the value of the car. So before you reaffirm a debt, make sure that payment is affordable and the car is in good shape!

Bankruptcy law gives you another option. As discussed in the Eighth Step, in Chapter 7, you could "redeem" the car by paying the fair market-value of the vehicle to the creditor rather than what you owe them. This is also a way of making amends. If you had surrendered the car and the creditor had sold it, they wouldn't have received more than fair market value anyway. There are lenders willing to work with folks in bankruptcy to help them accomplish this redemption.

Section 521 of the Bankruptcy Code requires that you surrender, reaffirm or redeem personal property on which there is a loan. However, it is silent as to real property. So in some jurisdictions (there is a split of opinion in the courts) a fourth possibility arises: If the collateral is your home or other land, you could choose to do what's known as a "ride through". This is the decision to just keep making payments but not reaffirm the debt. Without a reaffirmation, the creditor cannot report your faithful payment record to the credit reporting agency to help raise your credit score. On the other hand, if you are late with a payment, they can't report that either.

If you don't reaffirm your home mortgage but intend to

"ride through" and you later fall behind on your payments, the mortgage company can foreclose and take the property. But they cannot sue you for the difference between the value of the house and the balance due on the mortgage.

In Chapter 13, making amends is accomplished by making payments to a trustee who is appointed by the court to manage your case. The trustee uses your money to pay your creditors according to the plan you filed with the Court. Your plan can provide for you to catch up on your mortgage payments, pay for your car, pay past due taxes. You pay the things that have to be paid, and then debts like credit cards get what's left over.

At the end of the plan term you are debt free usually except for your mortgage, which you keep on paying. It isn't easy, but things were already way out of control in your finances. Life would have been even more difficult if you hadn't filed for protection under Chapter 13.

The Ninth Step of making amends is an important part of the personal growth available when we work the Twelve Step program. Making amends is when we take personal responsibility for our actions. We pay the debts we can pay – like the third line of the Serenity Prayer suggests:

> *God, grant me the serenity*
> *To accept the things I cannot change*
> *Courage to change the things I can*
> *And the wisdom to know the difference.*

(Taken from the full Serenity Prayer written by Reinhold Niebuhr)

Rise Like a Phoenix

Tenth Step – Maintenance of Good Financial Habits

Continued to take inventory of our financial activities, our debts and our assets and when we were making financial decisions that did not support our prosperity, promptly admitted it and changed course.

The first portion of the Tenth Step is taking the post-bankruptcy Debtor Education Course. This course is required in order to get your discharge and is a different course from the one you took in order to be eligible to file bankruptcy in the first place. Congress created it hoping that providing bankruptcy debtors with some financial education would prevent them from ending up in bankruptcy again.

In the Debtor Education Course there is great emphasis on learning to budget. Take this very seriously.

First, spend a month tracking your expenses. Put all your income into your personal checking account and make sure all of your expenditures come out of that same account.

Be sure to include your semi-annual expenses (divide by six then add one sixth to your monthly budget) or annual expenses, (divide by twelve and add one twelfth to your monthly budget.)

I have been helping clients do budgets for 25 years, but I have never seen an easier to use or more logical budgeting system than the one chosen by Senator Elizabeth Warren and her daughter, Amelia Warren Tyagi in their book *All Your Worth: The Ultimate Lifetime Money Plan* (Tyagi, 2005). They divide your spending into three areas; Must Haves, Savings and Wants. I invite you to use the forms in the Appendix of this book to create your budget.

Just because you are spending an amount now, doesn't mean you have to continue to have that same amount as a budget item. You can make adjustments, some of which are included in this Chapter on the Tenth Step.

This is the time for you to take control over your money rather than your money controlling you. Now that you are freed from paying for your past, develop a solid plan for investing in your future.

As you continue with your "Fresh Start" you need to watch yourself carefully to prevent backsliding into the spending habits that got you into trouble in the first place. Bankruptcy doesn't give you a fresh start if you continue to do things the way you used to.

A promise is a promise again:

1. If you reaffirmed a vehicle loan or other debt in your bankruptcy (promised to pay it just as if you had never filed), pay it every month. Pay it off. Don't give in to the temptation to surrender the collateral and stop paying. That said, there is a provision in the Bankruptcy Code for "rescinding" the reaffirmation agreement within 60 days of making the agreement or 60 days of your discharge, whichever is later. It is for very quick changes of heart. After that 60 days passes, you are "Sure out of luck". You must pay it off.

2. If you get a credit card after your bankruptcy:

   a. Use it for something like gas for the car and pay it off every month
   b. Show a history of responsible use.
   c. Do not start carrying balances again.
   d. Do not charge up the card over 50% of the credit limit. If possible stay down at 30% or less.

3. Pay your mortgage or rent on time every month. If you want to refinance your mortgage to get a better rate in the future, they aren't going to talk to you if you consistently run late. Besides, when you pay late, interest continues to accumulate on your loan, so that when you finally do make your payment, even more of your payment goes to interest than to principle. I've looked at enough mortgage loan histories for clients to see why they aren't making progress in paying down their loan. Late payments are usually the reason. If you are paying rent and want to buy

a house, the bank may well want to see a letter from your landlord showing how you pay your rent.

The Road to Financial Recovery

1. After you get your bankruptcy discharge, send a copy of your petition and order of discharge to each of the credit reporting agencies (sample letter in Appendix.)

2. Monitor your credit report to make sure that your debts are reported correctly.

3. Start saving. Your first goal should be to save $1000 cash in a safe in your home. In the event of weather emergency or other such disaster, having $1000 cash available could make the difference between feeding your family and going hungry. Then set aside three to six or even more months of household expenses in a savings account to protect yourself if you experience job loss.

4. If your employer has a 401k and matches funds, put at least the amount the employer will match in your 401k. Better yet, if you are able, start depositing the maximum allowable in your 401k.

5. Get a secured Visa or MasterCard. They are safer than only using a debit card. You only need one. Credit cards are insured against fraudulent use should someone steal your number and use your card. If your debit card number is stolen, the thief has direct access to your

bank account and unless you catch it within two days, the bank may not replace the funds when the fraud is discovered. Some banks have better policies to protect their customers, but it's best not   to chance it. I know too many people who have lost a lot of money from stolen debit cards/debit card numbers.

6. To establish a history of responsible use, use your card for gas or groceries and pay it off every month. Never charge it up over 50%, and better yet, never charge it up over 30%. As you can, apply for a higher limit by adding to your savings account.

7. If you are tempted to buy furniture you can't afford on credit, STOP! Save the money and wait, or look for something used that will serve your purpose and pay cash for it.

8. When an appliance breaks down, if it can't be repaired inexpensively buy a used appliance for a low price. There are stores that sell used appliances and give warrantees. Don't buy on time. You don't need another bill. And you'd be amazed what excellent appliances are being sold by people who are "redoing" their kitchens. Look on Craigslist!

9. Understand why you spend money. We all have reasons for why we spend – rich and poor alike. Do you spend more money on gifts because you wait to the list minute? I caught myself doing that. My excuse? "I'm too busy to plan ahead." So rather than planning ahead and getting something thoughtful that I can ship free or

inexpensively, I spend too much and then have to pay for express overnight shipping. And I'm sure I purchased a more expensive gift than I would have if I planned ahead. Do you shop when you're frustrated about something? Create a new way of taking care of yourself when you are under stress. Go for a walk. Watch a special movie or plan an evening with a friend.

10. When you are ready to purchase a home, look for one that costs less than the banks say you can afford. If you are married, pick a house that either you or your spouse could pay for on one of your salaries. Think about lease options. Make sure you can put down the 20% down payment so you don't have to pay for costly private mortgage insurance (PMI.)

11. *Don't co-sign a loan for anyone.* Not your parents or your children or a co-worker or a friend. No one.

12. I don't even recommend co-signing student loans for your children, though with student loan regulations being what they are, that may be difficult. I refused to co-sign a student loan for my son, Peter, that would have actually funded the more expensive lifestyle that he wanted to live; since he wanted to live away from home and he wanted to have a newer car which would require him to make car payments. "Fine, have it your way," I said. (Well, it may have taken me a while to get to "Fine.") "I'm not funding that choice and you need to work while you go to school." And so he worked all through college. He learned excellent time management skills, made very good grades,

found scholarships, and graduated without owing any student loan debt. And I didn't have his student loan debt either!

13. If you have a loan on your car, pay it off and keep driving it. Enjoy the feeling of having no car payment

14. If your car breaks down before you've paid it off, fix it and continue to pay it off. If you just cannot make the payments, talk to your lender about letting you sell it. If it doesn't sell for enough to pay off the loan, sign a note for the difference AND PAY IT!

15. Drive the paid off car until it just isn't fixable any more. Each month, even after the car is paid off, put the same amount into savings that you would have spent on a car payment. This way, you will have cash available to buy your next car outright!.

16. When it is finally time to buy another car, buy something you can pay cash for using the cash you saved. Get over worrying whether you look cool in it or whether it's the luxury car you deserve. Drive it while you save your "car payment" money so you can trade up next year for a better used car.

I have a confession to make, I get bored with cars. I've had car payments for the last 20 years. And I've lost a lot of money trading in cars on which I still owed money. But I've seen the light. My current car is a 12-year-old BMW convertible with standard transmission that I purchased used 5 years ago. Not a boring car. The price was reasonable and the payments were doable and I paid it off in 2015, about six months ahead of schedule. I'm keeping it. It's dependable and fun too. I'm committing to the world and all my readers that I'll save the payments so I can buy the next used car for cash. You read it here, folks!

To get control of your money, make some budget changes:

a. Modify your mortgage if you are eligible for a lower payment.

b. Compare car insurances and get the best rate possible.

c. Compare cell phone plans or get a pre-paid.

d. Reduce or eliminate cable or satellite TV.

e. Go to the public library instead of buying books and renting videos. The library is an amazing resource. Use it!

f. Do a small splurge on one lunch out a week. Make it special and enjoy it. Don't make it a daily habit you take for granted as you may have done before the bankruptcy.

g. Rather than meeting your friends at a bar for drinks, meet at one of your houses and each bring a bottle of wine or hors d'oeuvres. Fun at a fraction of the price and you can be as loud and obnoxious as you want without having to face the bouncer!

h. Take in a roommate and have them help with the expenses. If you have adult children living at home, they need to participate in the overhead or move out. And they need to pay their own car payments and insurance.

If you are still struggling consider the following:

a. Get a second job. Clean houses. Bag groceries.

b. Ask for overtime at your job.

c. If you have to stay home because you have young children at home, or physically just can't work more, look into work you can do at home, such as a telephone answering service where you can answer phones at home or help others by providing day care for their children and be paid for it.

d. Sell things in your house that you don't need. Craigslist is free. Use it to advertise for sale the furniture that you don't need that fills your attic, your garage or worse yet, a storage locker that you pay for monthly. Save that money.

e. If you are comfortable with sales, try network marketing. Watch carefully though to make sure you are making more money than the business costs you. I'm not a fan of rationalizing that it's good to show a loss in your business. Embrace profit!

f. If you lose your job, don't sit at home. Get some kind of work. Anything! It is always easier to find your right and perfect job if prospective employers can see that you are a "get it done" kind of person. And if you can't find any work at all, volunteer at the Red Cross, or the hospital auxiliary or the food bank. Be useful. You will feel better about yourself and prospective employers will feel better about you too.

Many people file bankruptcy swearing that they are "over" credit cards. They will never be in this situation again.

Some financial recovery teachers recommend against rebuilding your credit after bankruptcy. I disagree with them and encourage my clients to rebuild their credit carefully and learn to keep it under control. You CAN do this. For most of us, it's not the same as an alcoholic having a glass of champagne at a wedding. It's more like someone in recovery from food addiction learning to eat in a healthy way. In today's economy, having some ability to use credit in a healthy way is like eating in a healthy way.

I've been practicing in the same town long enough that I do see "repeat business." Good people who really did not expect that they would ever have to file another bankruptcy. Some of the reasons this happens are just part of the human condition:

1. Illness that interferes with their ability to work a full time job.

2. Family member who requires full time care.

3. Business failure.

4. Loss of employment.

5. Loss of a spouse.

6. Loss of a spouse's job.

7. Having purchased more house than they could maintain.

8. They co-signed a loan for someone who then didn't pay it.

If we set ourselves up for success right after bankruptcy by doing things differently like:

- Creating and sticking to a monthly budget
- Building a savings account
- Using a secured credit card responsibly and paying it off each month
- Having no car payments
- Having a house or rent payment that either spouse can handle on their own

Then life events like the ones listed above will be much more manageable.

The Tenth Step is about staying on course, continuing to take that fearless and searching inventory, and redirecting ourselves when we get off course. We can do this.

Rise Like a Phoenix

Eleventh Step – Learning More About Money

Sought through reflection and study to improve our knowledge of financial management, learning more about good financial stewardship, being careful to act in accordance with our best understanding of those practices.

One of my favorite experiences is running into former bankruptcy clients in the mall, for instance, and having them call me out and tell me how they are doing. One of my favorite couples to see periodically are "Debbie" and "Dan."

Debbie and Dan filed Chapter 7 bankruptcy in the mid 1990's. At the time, they were each working two full-time jobs to pay their bills and to pay for their dream home. The mortgage payment was half of their combined salaries from their four full-time jobs. In counseling them, I told them quite frankly that I thought they should give up their house in the bankruptcy. I was concerned that they couldn't continue to work like they were forever and that if they lost even one of their four jobs, they would lose their house!

But I didn't know this couple or their determination very well. Debbie and Dan had a vision – a dream. They were determined to realize that vision. They realized that using credit cards had nearly derailed them, and they determined that they weren't going to do that again. After the bankruptcy they continued to work their four full-time jobs and worked hard to pay off the mortgage on their dream home.

They had another dream that I didn't know about. They wanted to own their own business. While they were working their four jobs, they paid attention to how businesses are run and how they should be run. They saved their money and they opened a retail store.

I dropped by their store recently to shop and say hello. The store was bustling with customers, and Debbie and Dan were busy ringing up sales and answering questions. They only had a moment to talk to me. I was touched when Debbie turned to Dan and said "you know who this is, don't you? It's Kathryn. She was with us in our darkest hour." Dan leaned over and whispered to me, "You know we paid our house off – a long time ago!" Then they had to return to helping their many customers. Debbie and Dan are Phoenixes of the rare and powerful kind!

I recently receive this email from another former client – it made me cry!

Mrs. Hathaway,

Good morning. I wanted to follow up with you on something. 5 years ago I came into your office with my tail tucked between my legs. To say that I was scared and embarrassed would be an understatement.

The last 4 years I have followed and done everything you have told me to do. I got a new job (which I shared with you) and have been at this job for now over 4 years. I have built a pretty decent IRA, a pretty respectable savings account and have an updated credit score of 700. And last but not least I am finally closing on my new home next week. I wanted to share a picture with you to let you know my progress. Had it not been for you taking the time to meet with me and assist me with this and guide me in the right direction, I don't know what I would have done or where I would be right now.

THANK YOU FROM THE BOTTOM OF MY HEART!!!

John T

This is why I get up in the morning. My clients tell me initially that the required Debtor Education course was helpful, but later follow up indicates that just one course isn't enough. The financial habits that got us here are ingrained and well-practiced. It seems to me that it will take more than just one course to change the habits created over years and decades.

Rise Like a Phoenix

Twelfth Step – Pay It Forward

*Having had an awakening as the result of these steps,
we teach our children and others about financial
responsibility, and practice these principles in
all our affairs.*

People with long experience in recovery tell us that the most effective way to teach others the wisdom of the Twelve Steps is to live it yourself. And so it is with financial recovery. Talking the talk but not walking the walk doesn't make a very effective "evangelist" for any cause.

We create our budgets so that we can live within our means. We save 10 to 20% of our income for our future. We pay cash for our cars and set aside money for repairs.

By telling your children and your friends that you've turned over a new leaf and are living a life of financial responsibility, you find you have new "accountability partners." You have to walk your talk or they will most certainly tell you about it. You may say, "Don't take my inventory" but when we tell others about financial responsibility, we've opened the door to others calling us on our stuff. That's what accountability is about!

One of my personal heroes is Pam Maldonado. She never had any debt, but she didn't have any money either. She never let that stop her from raising her four children, always having enough, buying a house and saving money. In 1995 she found herself a single mother of four children, ages 4, 6, 7 and 9, without child support. Though she had earned a teaching degree, she had left teaching early to do what was most important to her – being a mom. Because she and her husband had negotiated a fifty-fifty time share with the children, she did not receive any child support after their divorce, though she still had to maintain a home for four children, feed and clothe them and provide medical care.

Early on, Pam made some important decisions that would guide her to making her situation a positive one. First she decided that she was not a victim and would never see herself that way. She focused on the positive in every situation. Early in her single years she was grateful that food stamps were available to help her feed her children. She was grateful that she found house cleaning and yard work to do while she looked for a teaching job so she could provide a home for her children. She was grateful for a duplex to rent for $525 per month.

In 1996, Pam's income was around $12,000 for the year.

In 1997, she was grateful that her income rose to $14,000. Every year she earned a little more. She finally crossed the $20,000 a year mark in 2003. Her first full time job was as a pre-school teacher.

Another decision Pam made was that she would not go into debt. No credit cards. She reasoned that at her income level she couldn't afford another bill! As a child she watched her parents argue about bills and money, and it left a bad taste in her mouth for debt. So when she got each paycheck she would pay the rent, utilities, car insurance and put a little in a savings account so when the car needed repairs or tires, she had the money already set aside. Even while earning less than $15,000 a year and supporting four children, Pam saved money.

Pam quickly learned that the least expensive way to manage transportation was to keep her paid for a 1980 twelve passenger van that she and her husband had bought for cash and fix it when it broke rather than thinking that she needed to trade it in for a car payment. When the children had grown up and bought their own vehicles, (with cash they had earned and saved!) she sold the van and purchased a new car for cash. Car payments had no place in her budget.

When the children were home, Pam planned meals with the children, taught them to look for sales and then shopped with them. When the children were with their father, she cleaned houses and did yard work and saved the money.

She provided health care using Florida's Healthy Kids program, which provides health insurance for children on a sliding scale. Pam was grateful for her own good health but did not have health insurance until she started her full time job at a private school. In the meantime, if she needed health attention she went to the health department which offered care and medicine on a sliding scale. Still no debt!

Pam paid it forward by sharing her good money habits with her kids. Her four children paid for their own college educations by doing well in school so they could earn scholarships and applying for grants – but no student loans. They learned to work and save money so they could buy their own cars for cash and pay for their own insurance, gas and car repairs. Pam was happy to have them live at home while they pursued their college educations. Today her children are responsible money managers and are thriving adults. Pam confesses that though her kids have credit cards, they pay them off each month.

Pam continues to pay it forward by sharing her story with my listeners on *Being the Phoenix: Ask the Expert* tele-class. She has shared her techniques with friends who ask for help and makes herself available to groups who want to hear her story. Pam's positivity and "can do" attitude are profoundly inspirational. You can hear her interview at www.bethephoenix.net/teleclass-12-22-15/teleclass-archive/. In fact – enjoy other interviews you will find on that page.

Being the Phoenix ® LLC

My way of paying it forward is my creation of Being the Phoenix® LLC, a brand designed to provide continued inspiration, education and tools to support us in changing our habits and ideas about money. In the 10 years since the passage of the Bankruptcy Abuse Prevention and Consumer Protection Act (BAPCPA), I still see "repeat business." While I'm glad my former clients feel comfortable coming back to me, I feel that somehow I failed them by not supporting their vision for their future better. The habits that created our financial disasters need to be changed by constant reinforcement and support. It is my hope that through the tele-classes, webinars, podcasts, books and programs, we will create a community of support people can turn to for ideas and inspiration.

You can find out more about Being the Phoenix by going to www.Bethephoenix.net. Download my free e-book, *The Phoenix's 7 Steps to Financial Recovery and Mastery*. Sign up to receive invitations and updates on the ongoing courses. We have an archive of interviews with experts including mortgage brokers, reverse mortgage specialists, tax experts, budgeting experts, successful network marketers, and other areas of interest to rising phoenixes.

If you have an idea for a class, please email me at KathrynHathaway@bethephoenix.net. The curriculum will expand with new offerings as needs become apparent.

The BethePhoenix.net website is a one stop shop for financial literacy with links to retirement planning calculators, the social security website and amortization calculators. We have books and videos addressing the needs of our members in our ever expanding library of resources. I'm not an expert in all these areas, but I know people who are.

I envision BethePhoenix.net becoming a growing community of support, an accountability group where we can share the trials and tribulations of reinventing our financial selves and share the triumphs and trailblazing as we transition into phoenixes, rising from the ashes of financial ruin.

Be the Phoenix

You can create a future of financial security. You have the power to change the habits and beliefs that led you to experience financial disaster. You have the right to experience abundance by learning new financial skills and habits. You can rise from the ashes of financial ruin. You can experience *Being the Phoenix* yourself.

Rising from the Ashes for Married People

If you are married, you and your spouse need to be on the same page regarding financial goals and plans.

1. This is a team sport. Do it together.

2. Figure out what your individual financial styles are – Spender or Saver.

3. Understand your financial situation from your partner's point of view.

4. If you decide to join an accountability group, you and your spouse should do it together if you can.

5. Have a joint bank account that you both put your paychecks into.

6. Give yourselves an allowance for gas money and a meal out occasionally.

7. Create a budget and live on it.

8. Pay bills together.

9. Talk about everything you want to spend money on.

10. Hold each other accountable.

11. Keep no secrets.

12. Laugh - A lot. Make it fun.

Conclusion

Financial Recovery is possible and you can do it. I am doing it with you.

I always try to help my bankruptcy clients develop a vision for their future that includes a vision for how they can create a savings plan, earn more money, pay off the debts that are not discharged, and build a positive financial future. But it was not until I faced my own second bankruptcy that it really hit home that talk simply is not enough. My first bankruptcy resulted from the collision of three failed marriages following on the heels of years as a single parent. In the end, creditors who filed claims received 95 percent of their money. But I could not pull off paying them in time to avoid the bankruptcy.

The second bankruptcy, about eighteen years later, I knew better. My credit card debt was very small, but two business loans, one of them a mortgage on my house, taken out in the last of the "boom" years, followed by the market crash in 2007–2009 made me feel like I had no choice but to file again. You would think that with the economy in tatters, bankruptcies would have increased. In fact, what happened was that people stopped paying their mortgages and used their money to pay their credit cards instead. Mortgage companies were not foreclosing very quickly, so folks who would have been my clients normally had years of peace and quiet before they needed me again. Bankruptcy filings all over the country declined, and I was not prepared for the shift. I suffered from lack of imagination and did not know where to turn.

In retrospect, I wish I had been more creative. I wish I

had had a community behind me like Women's Prosperity Network, a fabulous organization led by Nancy Matthews, Trish Carr, and Susan Wiener, established for the purpose of supporting women in learning business skills, creating profits, and getting real results; but I did not.

Since learning and implementing the strategies I have shared here and at BeThePhoenix.net, I have learned to be more creative. I have revived the profitability of my law practice, empowered my staff to do the same and am walking the path of financial mastery. I tell myself that the more embarrassing events of my life exist so that I can now empathize with anyone, anywhere. I have developed a very special empathy for people who have to file bankruptcy as well as for others working to recreate financial futures.

That is why I have created Being the Phoenix®, LLC, a community providing inspiration, education, and resources to support people in rising from the ashes. The website, www.BeThePhoenix.net, is growing with blog posts, articles, and an archive of teleclasses. Download our free eBook, *7 Steps to Financial Recovery and Mastery.*

Go now to BeThePhoenix.net to gain instant access.

Do you have a story of rising from the ashes? Would you like to share your success story with others and become a published author? Your story can inspire others as well as be a platform to share your business and expertise. Go to BeThePhoenix.net/book to start a conversation with me about your story.

"And Still I Rise"
~ Maya Angelou

About the Author

Kathryn A. Hathaway is a shareholder in Hathaway Sprague Law, P.A. and the Chief Visionary and Founder of Being the Phoenix®, LLC, which provides resources and support for rising from the ashes of financial ruin to claim the abundant life you are meant to live. She practices law in northern Florida and is board certified by the American Board of Certification as an expert in consumer bankruptcy law. With nearly thirty years of legal experience, including bankruptcy, probate, asset protection and estate planning, she is 100 percent committed to helping individuals rebuild their lives, despite financial challenges and setbacks. Kathryn looks not just to the situation at hand, but also assists clients in visualizing a better future on the other side of their current legal problem.

Most important, Kathryn is mother to Peter, Nana Kat to Austen and Sam, and Mama Kat to house cats Tiger Lily and Xena, and office cats Boris and Natasha Badenov.

Rise Like a Phoenix

APPENDIX

Budgeting

This budget is divided into three categories as suggested by Elizabeth Warren and Amelia Warren Tyagi in their book *All Your Worth:*. Divide annual, semi-annual or quarterly expenses by the appropriate number of months in order to create a monthly number.

Must haves – 50%

Wants – 30%

Savings/debt reduction 20%[iv]

Must Haves

Must Have Item	Your monthly amount	Avg. Amt. Per person Per month
Rent/mortgage		
Utilities average of last 3 months:		
Electric		
Fuel Oil		
Gas		
Water		
Sewer		
Basic phone		
Homeowners or renters insurance		
Taxes		
Medical out of pocket (including vision, dental, co-pays and prescriptions, Divide annual or bi-annual expenses into		$60

monthly budget expenses)		
Health Insurance		
Term Life Insurance (whole life goes under savings!)		
Disability Insurance		
Car insurance (if paid annually divide by 12, if paid semi annually divide by 6)		
Transportation- Gas, Oil, Repairs		$244/vehicle Less car insurance (limit 2 vehicles) $175 to $350/mo
Food v		
Legal obligations such as Such as car payment		
Legal Obligation		
Student loan		
Ongoing contractual payments such as cell phone contract, gym membership, child care, satellite, contracts paying for appliances or furniture (though I hope you got rid of those debts in your bankruptcy!)		
Child support or alimony		

Total Must Haves $_____

What percent is this number of your monthly income less taxes: _____%

Savings

Retirement Savings	$
Regular Savings	$
Whole Life Ins. (if you can get term instead, I recommend it)	$
Credit Card payments left over after bankruptcy.	$
Extra payments on your contract debt	$

Total Savings $_____

What percentage is this of you income less taxes?

_____ %

Wants

Want	Actual cost per month	Adjusted cost per month
Cable		
Clothing		
Gifts		
Vacations		
Entertainment		
Eating Out		
Manicures, pedicures, hair stylist		
Other non-necessities		

Total Wants Spending $_____

Percent of Income less taxes _____%

Corrections for over spending $_____

Adjusted Wants percentage _____%

Letter to Credit Reporting Agencies

Experian P.O. Box 2002 Allen, TX 75013 888-397-3742 www.experian.com	Trans Union (TU) P.O. Box 1000 Chester, PA 19022 800-888-4213 www.transunion.com
Equifax Credit Information Services P.O. Box 740256 Atlanta, GA 30374 800-685-1111 www.equifax.com	

Date

Re: Your name

    Your Social Security No._____

Gentlemen:

Enclosed you will find copies of my Voluntary Petition for Relief in Bankruptcy, along with my Schedules D, E, and F, Notice of Commencement (a/k/a 341 notice) and Discharge of Debtor.

Please update my credit report so that it shows that all these debts were discharged by my bankruptcy. Please send me a corrected copy of my credit report when the update is completed.

Thank you for your assistance in this matter.

Sincerely,

Your name & address

---

i Pay Day Loans – loans taken from lenders who loan you money literally until the next payday. They accept a check from you dated for your next pay day, which they will deposit on that day. Or, better for them, you can renew the loan at the payday for 10% of the loan. You literally pay 10% interest every two weeks or 520% per year. Payday loans are big business online operating out of countries like Malta and Nigeria. They take your payment directly from your bank account – with your permission, no less! And because they aren't governed by U.S. laws, their interest rates can be astronomical!

ii Chapter 13, commonly known as the Wage Earner's Debt Consolidation (11 U.S.C. § 1301 et seq.) is a powerful tool to rehabilitate mortgages, cram down to fair market value other secured debt, and strip off entirely unsecured second mortgages. In Chapter 13 you pay extra your creditors. Cram down means to pay the secured creditor the fair market value of the property through the plan instead of the larger balance on the loan.

iii The Home Affordable Refinance Program (HARP) was established by the Federal Housing Finance Agency in 2009 to help homeowners who have been unable to get a traditional refinance because declining home values have made the home worth equal or less than the balance due on the mortgage. The homeowner must be current in payments. The program has been expanded to assist homeowners who are struggling and is extended through the end of 2016. Find more information at www.harp.gov.

iv *All Your Worth: The Ultimate Lifetime Money Plan*, Elizabeth Warren and Amelia Warren Tyagi Free Press (a division of Simon & Shuster) 2005.

v The USDA website has charts showing proposed budgets for individuals of all ages and families showing what families should spend for food from a thrifty plan, low cost, moderate cost and liberal plan should cost. I've shown the range per person here, but you can obtain more updated or exact information by going to
http://www.cnpp.usda.gov/USDAFoodPlansCostofFood/reports.